Grandparents Raising Grandchildren

Supergrands and Their Superkids

Barbara Setzer

Published by LULU Press
860 Aviation Parkway, Suite 300
Morrisville, NC 27560

ISBN Number: 978-0-557-00647-2
Library of Congress Control Number: 2008908540

Preface

Grandparents of middle age or older may be assuming a major care giving role in raising their grandchildren due to the parents inability to raise their children because of family crisis. At a time when retirement and a slower pace of life is a primary concern to the grandparents they are called upon to become a surrogate parent. The family's biological unit needs to be maintained and the grandparents normal "pleasure without responsibility" (Dillman-Jenkins, Blankemeyer, & Olesh, 2002, p. 219) is turned ninety degrees to total responsibility.

It is particularly important to note before reading this "that the National Institutes of Health summarizes the state of grandparenting research as incomplete, atheoretical, and often neglecting the roles of gender, age, social class, and ethnicity" (Kelch-Oliver, 2008, p. 44).

To all grandparents, and their grandchildren whom this book is sincerely dedicated to.

Thanks to
Dr. Donna Wagner for her patience and encouragement, and to Dr. Phyllis Freeman for her encouragement.

Contents

1 Introduction   1

2 Why Do Grandparents Care for Their Grand-   5
  children?

3 Background   8

4 Reasons for Grandparent Custody   11

5 The Effects of Caring for a Grandchild on   16
  Older People

6 Child's Point of View   21

7 Grandmother vs. Grandfather   23
  as a Caregiver

8 Effects on Absent Children   26

9 Needs of the Grandparents Raising   28
   Grandchildren

10 Policy Analysis and Recommendations   44

   References   48

Introduction

The trend of grandparents raising grandchildren is growing rapidly, to the extent that grandfamilies have captured the interest of policy makers, researchers, and advocates. An issue that was once private is now public and very intergenerational (Smith, Beltran, Butts, & Kingson, 2000).

"A national study of grandparents raising grandchildren found that more than one in ten grandparents are at some point responsible for rearing grandchildren for six months or more" (Smith & Beltran, 2000, pp.7-8). According to the 2005 American Community Survey, there are 6,706,706 children across the United States and its' territories under the age of 18 that are actively being raised by their grandparents with or without biological parents present. These children are relatives (The grandparents' children's child), fictive kin (feelings of identification between two or more people, such as godparents or family friends of the child), or step grandchildren (according to Szinovacz this is 20-25% of the grandparents raising their grandchildren, p.40). Grandparents are "involving themselves and possibly taking over custody of their grandchildren and providing most of the child's care" (Force, Bottsford, Pisano, & Holbert, 2000, p.5).

Many articles call the growth of grandfamilies a phenomenon such as "...leading to potential underestimates of this phenomenon" (Szinovacz, 1998, p.37). According to the 2006 Oxford English Dictionary (p 1280), "A phenomenon is a fact or event that appears, or is perceived, by one of the senses or the mind, especially, one whose cause or explanation is in question." Calling grandfamilies a phenomenon is pulling the situation out of context and making it appear as unusual. Grandparents, especially, in the Afro-American and Hispanic race have been raising their grandchildren since time immemorial (Minkler & Fuller-Thomson, 2005).

Some of the articles that were written in the 90's inferred and emphasized, by pointing an accusing finger and blaming, calling parents irresponsible (a label) if they cannot raise their own children. Such as, "...the main cause, however, is a parent's substance abuse. A grandparent raising a child is because the parent is dealing with substance abuse" (Kluger & Aprea, 1999, p. 6). Or, "Literature reveals that substance abuse is the most common precipitating factor related to grandmothers' becoming surrogate caregivers" (Fitzgerald,

2001, p. 298) Parents can become incapacitated because:

- They are HIV positive.
- Enrolled in drug treatment programs.
- Perpetrators of sexual or psychological abuse.
- Incarcerated
- Substance abuser
- Alcohol abuser
- Parental abuse and neglect towards the children.
- Divorce, "The rising divorce rate adds to a complex family structure" (Szinovacz, 1998, p. 39).
- Children having children or out-of-wedlock births.

In reality, the reason as to why the child is placed with the grandparents can be unpredictable and exemplary such as:

- One or the other parent or both dies or is very sick emotionally, psychologically or physically.
- Either parents or one parent goes to war and does not return or returns severely disabled. This leaves the other parent financially challenged and a caregiver to a child and a spouse.
- A child of a drug addicted mother. Many drugs cross the placenta (such as cocaine) and the baby is born an addict also. This is considered to be child abuse (in utero substance abuse). Child welfare places the baby with the biological surrogate grandparents or kin.

- Abandonment-the baby in the dumpster, and, the baby left on the doorstep is still prevalent. Leaving an infant under two months unsupervised and unprotected in a public or private setting for an extended period of time with intention of abandoning the baby is considered child abandonment.
- Illness and death from HIV/AIDS. The parent does not necessarily abuse drugs (by sharing needles) or have multiple sex partners. The parent could have had an operation and received tainted blood in the transfusion.
- Victim of sexual or physical violence.
- A child's developmental or emotional needs which demands special attention, education, or the child welfare agency.

"Regardless of how the arrangement came about all children living with their grandparents have experienced a separation from a parent which can be traumatic. Yet, research suggests that living with a relative, rather than with a nonrelative or in an institution, may minimize this trauma by providing the child with a sense of family support" (Scarcella, Macomber, & Geen, 2003, p.1). Once a grandchild is with their grandparent "more than 50% of the children are with their grandparents for three years or more" (Policy Brief, January, 2007, p.3).

2

Why Do Grandparents Care for Their Grandchildren?

Grandparents are emotionally and psychologically moving beyond their own needs to maintain the valuable family unit. It is not a new phenomenon for a grandparent to intervene or assist in raising their grandchildren or other relatives (Mills, Smith, & DeLeon, 2005, p. 192). The grandparents have to hold off retirement plans, health issues, financial issues and any family dynamics such as the grandparents' child's failure as a parent and the grandparents' failure as a parent. The National Survey of American Families data suggests that for most children arrangements are made privately within the family (Scarcella, Macomber, & Geen, 2003).

Grandparents do not accept foster care because the biological grandchild is being raised by a stranger and the grandparents want the grandchildren to be raised within the biological family unit. Also, grandparents do not believe that once they become entangled in the "...formal child welfare system the agency will respect the grandparents cultural values about termination of parental rights or adoption" (Smith & Beltran, 2000, p. 11).

Grandparents need to protect their rights and obtain legal guardianship or custody. Without either legal action the grandparents power is rendered useless if the parents come back to get the children (and the parents rights have not been legally terminated).

The grandparent's biological ties to their grandchildren are what keep family cohesiveness. To a young child under 6 years of age (which is the majority age group) [2000 United States Census Bureau; Smith and Beltran, 2000] this strong cohesive bond is the basis of a secure relationship between grandparent and child. Grandparents want this bonding to their grandchild to continue and flourish. It gives the grandparents a great sense of purpose and pride. According to Generations United (2002, p.iii), "Grandparents and other relatives who step forward to raise children are providing an invaluable service to their families and our country."

To further the cohesiveness intergenerational communication enriches both children and grandparent and completes a viable solution and refuge to both contrasting generations in times of need and in the future as the "bookend generations" (Generations United, 2002, p. 1).

Grandparents provide a crucial safety net for these children. The grandparents should have public aid (financial, food, and medical) readily available to them so they are able to cope with raising their grandchildren and meet his/her needs.

3

Background

In societies outside of the United States "the nature of grandparenthood varies with a multiplicity of cultural demographic, social, economic, psychological and historical factors" (Kivnick & Sinclair, 1996, p.611). However, in American society a grandparents' role is inferred to be of occasional visits to the grandchildren when any conflicts occur or provide temporary childcare. Their role is traditional and non-care giving.

The grandparent in American society is removed from a rigid structural role so their role is more gratifying then with the sanctions of a more formal society (Kivnick & Sinclair, 1996).

Unfortunately, that is not always the case in today's society. The nuclear family is fragmenting due to the individuals who make up the family unit. Those individuals are brought up from an early age to be independent. "The American family is rooted in indi-

vidualism" (Kivnick & Sinclair, 1996, p.613). Whatever issues there are concerning families today are not
unique to today's society. Family dynamics are different for each and every situation.

For whatever reason, the parents are incapable of
raising their biological children-so in steps the grandparent. To the grandparent the children need stability
and continuity as well as a biological family member.

In some ethnic groups such as the African-
Americans for a grandparent to assume full responsibility for grandchildren and provide most of their care is a
"long tradition". African-Americans are "rooted in
West African extended family traditions" (Minkler, &
Fuller-Thomson, 2005, p. s83). During times of slavery
when families were intentionally pulled apart, the
grandparents became the main caregiver of the children. Also, during the early part of the 20th century
when parents sought employment up north, children
were left to be raised by their grandparents. Because of
the African-American culture throughout time they are
able to adjust and adapt to preserve the family unit
more than any other cultural group in the United States
(Kelch-Oliver, 2008). "Three times as many African-
Americans children are being raised by grandparents
compared to their White peers" (Dillman-Jenkins,
Blankemeyer, & Olesh, 2002, p.221).

These "skipped generation families" (Mills, Gomez-Smith & DeLeon, 2005, p.193) are growing in
society at an ever increasing rate and are evolving into
a whole new trend. These grandparents that care for
their grandchildren are moving in a progressive direc-

tion that does not currently fit into societal norms.

4

Reasons for Grandparent Custody

Custody, according to the 2000 United States Census Bureau, is only sought by 20% of care giving grandparents. The reasons can be variable as discussed in the 'Introduction' of this paper. Child welfare agencies will remove the child or children from the home repeatedly, but will not really address the current issue(s), neither do the courts. The parents' abusive behavior will not go away. The dysfunctional behavior will only continue. No child needs to be raised by strangers or to be used as a tennis ball lobbed back and forth between abusive parents and an institution (foster care). To make matters worse abuse of a child, in most cases, falls under a misdemeanor. As a result the abuser does not take his or her sentence seriously. Thus the pattern of dysfunction continues.

Many grandparents are aware of this social problem and will take their children to court to gain custody. Or, child welfare agencies will place the child with an adult relative whenever it is possible as a "first foster care option" (Fitzgerald, 2001, p.297). The grandparent is not going to tolerate their child's dysfunctional behavior. The grandparent will go as far as proving the parents unfit in court to gain custody. This is often a traumatic step but a forced issue by the courts (Statistics for Grandparents Raising Grandchildren, 2008, p1). Many states have parental preference laws where "the parent has a constitutionally protected liberty and interest in the care, custody and control of his or her child" (Geer, 2007, p.1). Any legal procedure from visitation to custody considers 'the best interest of the child'. Some states are very specific about spelling out grounds for termination of parental rights and other states are very general in their use of language to set statutory grounds for involuntary termination of parental rights.

Another issue is that the grandparent can be on Social Security and a fixed income. Therefore, it becomes difficult to the grandparent to gain custody .The grandparent cannot prove to the judge that he or she can monetarily provide for the child (AARP, 1996-2008).

Grandparents may be frustrated at how the biological grandchild is being raised. There may be issues over discipline. Or the child is a special needs child who has "unmet developmental or emotional needs" who needs special education or a child welfare agency'' aide (AARP, 1996-2008).

Key Issues Involved in Surrogate Parenting by Grandparents

- If the grandparent raises the grandchildren informally the biological parent can return for the children and this usurps the grandparents' authority. In turn this creates trauma to both the grandparent and child.
- Because a grandparent is caring 24/7 for a grandchild, to maintain personal balance, the grandparent is going to need respite services. The grandparent needs time to themselves to step away from the situation and breathe. Then when the grandparent returns they can resume their job with a fresh outlook. This is not always the case, and a burnout can occur to the grandparent.
- A grandparent who is poor and a child on a TANF 'child only grant' forces the grandparent to receive temporary help but neither grandparent can fulfill the work requirement after receiving the benefits.
- Grandparents are looked down upon in the family when they need the emotional and psychological support of the biological unit. Everyone in the family is suddenly 'too busy'.
- Grandparents need to be seen and respected in society for what they do. Society does not shun a young mother. Both young mother and grandparent are raising children-what is the difference?

- The grandparent needs to reach out and know she or he can obtain information from a consistently reliable source so they can cope with the children and the demands of raising a child (or two). This knowledge empowers the grandparent so she or he can focus on raising the children.

- Grandparents raising grandchildren do not have accessibility to the children's medical, dental, or mental health records so the children can go to school. The grandparents cannot acquire medical services for the children nor can they acquire food stamps for the extra burden on the food budget, and they will have difficulty obtaining monetary help. Emotionally and psychologically the grandparents are shut out of obtaining these services because of the lack of legality between children and surrogate parent (grandparent). "Grandparents need to access necessary services for their grandchildren, such as school enrollment, immunizations, and medical treatments" (Smith, Beltran, Butts, & Kingson, 2000, p.90).

- When a grandparent seeks custody of a child it can be an arduous task. Many states have parental preference laws which mean the grandparent has to legally battle the parent and prove to the court that the parent is unfit. This type of legal action is a very traumatic step. What of those elderly on a fixed income? The grandparents are going to need money for legal matters and custody.

- Grandparents raising grandchildren alone or as a couple may not want to tell the truth on surveys because in their perception certain questions may be a threat to themselves or their grandchild's welfare. An example would be asking about the grandparent's health. Grandparents do not want the children taken away so the grandparent is going to overcompensate. This leads to a false-positive answer.

- The sudden onset of grandfamilies is not a phenomenon. "…Grandparents who are the primary caregivers of their grandchildren are not a modern day phenomenon" (Kelch-Oliver, 2008, p. 44). Phenomenons are exceptional or extraordinary events and there is nothing exceptional about families in crisis. Grandparents raising grandchildren have occurred throughout history. "It is not a new phenomenon for a grandparent to intervene or assist in raising their grandchildren or other relatives" (Mills, Smith, & DeLeon, 2005, p. 192).

- Much emphasis is placed upon a grandparent's formal educational level. This is completely invalid because education cannot be only registered by IQ alone. There is an education no formal school or college can teach. Education is not a tangible commodity. There is wisdom from experiences an older adult possesses that cannot be measured. The societal label has no bearing on the success or failure of the grandparents raising their grandchildren.

The Effects of Caring for a Grandchild on Older People

The effects of caring for a biological grandchild on older people, can be abrupt, and at first devastating. In 1998, according to the United States Census Bureau, "888,000 grandparent families cared for their grandchildren...Without either biological parent living in the household" (Smith & Beltran, 2000, p. 8). In 2005 approximately 2,458,806 grandparents had primary responsibility caring for their grandchildren (Children's Welfare League, 2007). Grandparents are psychologically, emotionally, and physically ready to slow down life's hectic pace, maybe retire and enjoy life's pleasures such as traveling, enjoying grandchildren when they want to, enjoy each other as companions, leisurely enjoying hobbies, sports, or learning and just taking life as it comes. These grandparent caregivers range in age between their 30's to their 80's. The chart below summarizes the 2000 U.S. Census Bureau results of how many grandchildren were raised in what grandparent age group:

30 to 39	-	269,694
40 to 49	-	1,360,278
50 to 59	-	1,824,500
60 to 69	-	1,378,378
70 to 79	-	733,440
80 and over	-	250,381

"Data is unspecified about the number of grandparents caring for more than one child" (Smith, & Beltran, 2000, p. 8). The grandparents may have unresolved issues with anger and resentment toward their own children (not being able to raise their biological child). Raising the children puts the grandparent in a "time disordered role" (Smith and Beltran, 2000, p.7) as if the grandparent was going back in time and living between time zones. The grandparent does not even have time to mourn the loss of the grandparent role, let alone, the perceived failed parent role from raising their own children.

Grandparents have to cope with any emotional, psychological, or physical problems the child brings into the household. Thus, the child will have health, behavioral, and educational issues.

Many grandparents make private arrangements with their children to care for their grandchildren. Because of this reason many grandparents do not accept services or aid from public agencies. They feel there is a stigma involved if they accept any public assistance.

Many of these grandparents could already be living in poverty and are not financially prepared for the extra burden upon their fixed incomes. Those caregivers between their 30's to their and 50's are not eligible for Social Security and other senior services that could help their primary role to the grandchildren (Dellman–Jenkins, Blankemeyer, & Olesh, 2002, p 221). Both male and female grandparents between the ages of 50 to 64 will maintain their jobs and "48 percent will work outside of the home" (Smith and Beltran, 2000, p. 10).

Grandmother is the main caregiver, who is working and may have to cut her hours at work, pass up promotions, and may eventually have to stop working to care for the grandchildren. This cuts her off from socialization with her peers. Without social, emotional, familial, and financial supports; depression could set in. "The notable feature of being a strong woman is that many grandmothers felt that they had to minimize their own health concerns in order to accomplish the surrogate task" (Fitzgerald, 2001, p. 299). This statement tells of how undervalued a grandmother feels when taking on this role as surrogate care giving parent. "Not only have more females added care of the grandchild to their productive and reproductive roles, but, in addition these efforts tend to be both invisible and undervalued" (Smith, Beltran, Butts & Kingson, 2000, p 86). Grandmothers will raise their biological grandchildren at any cost.

The grandparents want to see the grandchildren through to the completion of high school (Fitzgerald, 2001, p. 300). Other grandparents worry about living long enough to raise their grandchildren to adulthood. Still, others are concerned about "keeping up with a grandchild socially and physically in daily activities" (Kivnick & Sinclair, 1996, 617).

The difference in ages between the children and grandparents leave a tremendous communication gap. At a time when communication is crucial, there is very little free exchange of ideas. Of course all of this is contingent upon how the grandparent-grandchild relationship was prior to the grandparent becoming a surrogate parent. Grandparents need to be resourceful and creative to keep the lines of communication open and gently guide the child in discipline.

For grandparents who are the biological surrogate parents to their grandchildren, the effects of stress are well known. Stress can lead to all types of health problems such as myocardial infarction, strokes, high blood pressure, obesity, arthritis, diabetes, alcoholism, etc. "Surrogate grandparents have higher odds of experiencing ADL (activities of daily living such as, bathing, dressing, eating ,ambulating, and personal hygiene or toileting) limitations" (Mills, Gomez-Smith & DeLeon, 2005).

Many grandparents tend to ignore their health because of the lack of supports such as daycare, respite care, or adequate medical coverage that enables the grandparents to go to their own doctor's appointments (Smith & Beltran, 2000). "Grandmothers are found to underestimate their own health problems because of their intense desire to protect their grandchildren" (Dellman-Jenkins, Blankemeyer & Olesh, 2002, p.1). The grandmother is afraid that her grandchildren might be placed in a foster home if they are unable to care for them.

Yet, not all changes for grandparents are negative. New friendships can develop from mothers in a similar situation. Many grandparents can actually have improved health due to better diets and more vigorous activity with the grandchildren. Those grandparents who are dissatisfied with how they raised their children get a second chance. The grandparent has a sense of purpose in a society that devalues, dissociates, and isolates the elder. For all biological surrogate grandparents there is no replacement for the love and affection of a grandchild. What a grandparent gives, and, how they give and care for their grandchildren comes back to the grandparent when they need care - at least in theory.

6

Child's Point of View

How is a child affected when grandparents become the main caregivers? A child who is in the care of grandparents at an early age can be confused because the children do not understand why the biological parents(s) are not there. Separation from a parent can be traumatic (Scarcella, Macomber & Geen, 2003, p.1). Every child's adaptation to their grandparents is different. No two situations are alike. How the grandchildren and grandparents relate is dependent upon how their relationship was before the grandparent became the functional surrogate parent. Suddenly the grandchildren's grandparents are disciplinarians, and not as leisurely and relaxed as they once were. The traumas encountered by the children can leave them less trusting and more defiant, thus, psychiatric and developmental problems can occur. Grandparents have to develop highly resourceful parenting skills to help the child succeed in school, at home, and in life (Edwards, 2003, p. 206).

The children's surrogate parents may be on a fixed income and the children add an extra burden on an already stretched household budget. So the children are more likely to live in poverty. The children are affected because there is a housing, food, and medical insecurity and there is a lack of community services that are needed.

The children who are affected the most are under six years old (51%) according to the 1997 United States Census Bureau. Twenty-nine percent are six to eleven and 20% are twelve to seventeen, and of the six million children living with grandparents, 2.5 million are living without either parent present.

7

Grandmother vs. Grandfather
as a Caregiver

A grandparent's sex directly affects grandparenting style. One article explained that "...grandmothers were found to be more likely than grandfathers to have warm relationships with their grandchildren, to see themselves as a parent surrogate to their grandchildren, to make themselves accessible, to interact with their grandchildren and to find greater satisfaction in grandparenthood. Grandfathers...held a narrower view of what they had to offer grandchildren, had less intimate relationships with grandchildren, and were at risk for becoming the forgotten grandparent" (Somary & Stricken, 1998, p. 58). Another article states "grandmothers derive more satisfaction from grandparenting than do grandfathers" (Kausler & Kausler, 1996, p19). These types of statements belittle and discredit the efforts and love grandpa gives to his grandchildren. Men perceive love and care of a grand-child differently than a woman. That does not mean that grandfather's love less or get less satisfaction. Another damaging statement, "There is significant evidence that grandmothers as opposed to grandfathers take on most of the responsibility of surrogate parenting" (Fitzgerald, 2003, p. 299). This statement assumes two grandparents are raising the grandchildren. What about the grandfather who is raising the grandchildren alone? The 1997 U.S. Census Bureau survey revealed that 6% of the 3.9 million grandparent headed households was a grandfather only household. Since 1997 this figure has increased 36% (2005 U.S. Census Bureau American Community Survey).

The grandfather is 66% more likely to be gainfully employed and less likely to be poor (12%) and own his own home (81%) as opposed to women who have jobs (51%) and own homes (69%).

It is safer to say that grandmothers and grandfathers each have their own parenting styles by approaching the subject of raising grandchildren, as well as their own children, differently. Hopefully, the grandparents are in the same household raising grandchildren. Their individual styles are in complement to one another when raising their grandchildren.

According to the 1997 U.S. Census Bureau grandmother only households are 669,000 of the 3.9 million across the country. However, the American Community Survey for 2005 has grandmother head of households increasing to 64%. In these households the grandchildren are libel to be poor and in need of public assistance (food stamps, and financial aid) and uninsured (the child needs Medicaid, Medicare or SCHIP). Steady or full-time employment is scarce. Even if the grandmother does have a full-time job she may have to cut back hours or stop working to give full attention to the raising of her grandchildren (Casper and Bryson, 1998).

Both males and females living under the poverty line were equally using public assistance, as well as, free reduced lunches. They were also likely to live in crowded conditions (Minkler & Fuller-Thompson, 2005).

Those households that are run by both grandparents were 32% of the 3.9 million grandchildren across the nation (1997 U.S. Census Bureau).

Whether grandfather headed households, grandmother headed households, or both grandparents, raising the grandchildren in the environment with a relative, "remains fairly stable throughout the rest of the life course" (Kivnick and Sinclair, 1996, p. 616). "Anthropologist Margaret Mead maintains that intergenerational family relationships, exemplified by grandparenthood are absolutely essential to the child's development of his or her own uniqueness, wholeness and cultural and historical continuity" (Kivnick & Sinclair, 1996, p. 20).

Effects on Absent Children

No studies have been done on the effects on absent children. This would be a very effective study because breaking up a family is like tearing limbs from a body. The family unit becomes fragmented and becomes seriously dysfunctional.

Unless siblings are involved as a daily consistent danger to one another there can be no rationale to separating siblings. Usually, if one child is endangered, they are all removed and put into foster care. Siblings are not broken up and they are adopted as siblings. If they were separated they would grow up ambivalent towards one another. Each child will want the situation of the other and doubt will always cause 'sibling rivalry'.

If one child cannot be raised by the parents because of behavioral issues and the parents feel the child is incorrigible the parents will ask the grandparents to step in.

If all the children in a household are exposed to harm, child welfare will remove all of the children and the children will be placed with the biological grandparents or a relative.

"Grandfamilies tend to enable siblings to stay together and maintain contact with family members" (Policy Brief, 2007, p1).

9

Needs of the Grandparents Raising Grandchildren

The grandparents' needs are first and foremost their health. If their health is not maintained, it will decline markedly. Keeping up with the raising of one child, or more as a surrogate parent, requires emotional, psychological, and physical stamina.

Stress is probably the first and most continual problem that needs to be dealt with. If not dealt with effectively, stress can lead to a multiple of health and mental health issues. It sounds like an impossible feat but balance is what the grandparent needs to maintain. This can be achieved through exercise, seeking emotional support, or a spiritual connection. Grandparents need to access information immediately to:

- Counseling or mental health
- Recreation opportunities
- Parents groups

- Transportation
- Financial assistance (including foster care subsidies from the state's Department of Children and Family Services).
- Respite care
- Day care

Chart: Kluger and Aprea, 1999

Grandparents need respite care whether from a family member, babysitter, or hired help, so they are able to keep their doctors appointment and go on errands or just have time for themselves.

Having familial support can help encourage the grandparents in support, emotionally and psychologically cope with the role of surrogate parent more easily, and "individuals make available effective assistance to others in their social network" (Edwards, 2003, p 211). Unfortunately, many grandparents do not receive the support they need and they are isolated from their peers. The support groups offered for grandparents raising grandchildren is a good place to start this journey. Grandparents can network to find other grandparents raising grandchildren

- Grandparents raising their grandchildren are not respected as a surrogate parent. Yet, society dotes on mothers to be and mothers with young children. Young parents are obviously given understanding and are nudged into their role as 'mother' by society's' cooperation and support. Supportive information is also offered to young mothers in an accessible way. However, if a grandparent is raising a grandchild, society shuns and turns away from the grandparent, and sometimes the child. The grandparent is out of place, according to society. Could this be age discrimination?

Grandparents need to enroll their grandchildren in school. Many grandparents are caring for their grandchildren informally. Some states require a caregiver to have legal custody or guardianship and others do not. Our own state of Maryland has educational consent laws where an informal caregiver can submit the same affidavit to enroll the child in school. The affidavit allows consent to the child's medical treatment. Fourteen states have educational consent laws, 22 states have power of attorney laws (where parents can delegate relatives with the power of attorney for the care of their children). Still other states get caught up in the semantics of a federal regulation that distinguishes between surrogate parent and parent. This type of disconnection creates confusion.

Grandparents need a safe haven for themselves and their grandchildren. Housing problems arise when a grandchild comes into the household. Many housing units for the elderly do not allow long term additions. Also, certain size apartments only allow a specific amount of people to occupy it. If a grandchild moves in, this could endanger the grandparents' occupancy allowance. Then the grandparents could be evicted. Housing that is specific for grandfamilies needs to be available, such as Grandma's House in Los Angeles, CA or Grandfamilies House in Boston, MA.

Grandparents need financial assistance even if only for the child. The following is a list of possibilities:

- TANF (Temporary Assistance for Needy Families) child only grant.
- Social Security Income-if the child is physically, mentally, or psychologically challenged.
- Social Services-if the child is in the custody of the grandparents.
- Adoption Subsidy-if the grandparents adopt the child.
- Child support can come from both parents if they are not legally terminated as parents; they are financially responsible for the children.

Grandparents need guidance and support whether they are informal caregivers or formal caregivers. If they are caring for their grandchildren informally, parents still have custody of the child. The parents can always come and take their child. This completely disrupts the child's routine, as well as, the grandparent's. Informal care giving is the "vast majority of children living outside of their parents' home" (Olsen, 2008, p.1).

The grandparents do not want to seek legal action because the grandparent believes the care giving situation is only temporary and the grandparent does not want to get into a legal battle with their own child.

In a formal situation the courts can place the child into legal custody of the child welfare agency and the grandparent provides full-time care - a safety net and a permanency for the children.

On the more positive side, because legislation calls for the preferences of placing the grandchild with the grandparents or relatives, more children are placed with kin rather than foster homes (Smith & Beltran, 2000).

"Researchers, public policy makers and the media first began to notice the huge increase in grandparent maintained households around 1990" (Casper & Bryson, 1998, p. 2). It was not long after that the Senate and the House of Representatives began to focus on this issue (also, before the Select Committee on Aging in 1992). The hearings began to concentrate on policy inadequacies concerning grandparents raising their grandchildren.

Any community and support services are not easily accessed and the quality of services differs from state to state. Our fragmented system seriously hurts those in need (in this case the grandchild), as well as, those who are trying to help, the grandparent.

Because of the disjointed system, this makes it extremely difficult for the grandparents to navigate for services needed.

Grandparents' need to gain ready access to:
- Support or self help groups
- Counseling and mental health services
- Recreational opportunities
- Parents groups
- Transportation
- Financial assistance

- Respite care
- Day care
- Information and referral to services that will help in supporting the children in the current home

Chart: Kluger & Aprea, 1999

Some states have created ways to establish legal guardianship for grandparents. Still other states have created kinship navigator programs allowing grandparents to have access to community and support services. There are 3 states in the nation that have progressive navigator programs that are the forerunners for the United States.

- In Ohio H.B.130 supports extended family responsibility for the raising of Ohio's children. "This bill provides power of attorney to consensual grandparents who anticipate the birth parents to reacquire their children. And the Grandparent Caretaker Affidavit provides legal documentation when the biological parents cannot be found" (Reidelbach, 2004).
- New Jersey's Kinship Navigator program helps caregivers seek those services needed through information and referral that spans a wide range of needs for the caregiver. Such as cash assistance, child support, educational services, support services, etc.
- Washington State, like New Jersey, has a kinship navigator program that is not as refined as New Jersey's but they offer support groups and a

33

downloadable list of all navigator programs within the state.

Policies that concern the Social Security Act of 1935, Medicare. Medicaid, Child Welfare, SCHIP, Older persons and other related policies are in the form of a chronological list. This will provide a possible explanation for the inception and continuing growth of policy in this area:

- In 1935 under Title V (P.L.106-501) of the Social Security Act-This legislation provided for restrictive funds for child welfare services. A state allotment depended upon the population under 21 as compared to other states per capita income (CWLA, 2008).
- From 1936 to 1969 welfare became a very necessary program for poor mothers. The amount of families receiving welfare expanded from 162,000 in 1936 to 1,875,000 in 1969. This program was funded by the Social Security Act of 1935 as Aid to Families with Dependent Children (AFCD). AFDC was unable to keep up with the demand and inflation. Between the years of 1970 to 1994 a typical state AFDC benefits for a family of three fell 45% after adjusting for inflation (Frolick, 1999).
- In 1965, President Lyndon Johnson supported and Congress enacted the Medicare Program. This program is designed as a federally subsidized healthcare insurance plan for the elderly, disabled and those with end-stage renal disease.

The program is run by the Department of Health and Human Services.

- Medicare provides 'reasonable and necessary' health insurance under:
  - Part A-the hospital insurance component that provides for skilled nursing care, hospice care, hospital care and other services. This is paid for through the Social Security tax.
  - Part B-a supplementary medical insurance that one has to pay for from the Social Security checks that provides for doctor's fees, outpatient hospital visits and other medical services that are not covered by Part A.
  - Part C (Medicare Advantage)-this plan is contingent upon a person having Parts A and B. This plan allows individuals to have care from a provider organization. Extra benefits are available but cost more money.
  - Part D was signed into law by President Bush on December 8, 2003 as the Medicare Prescription Drug Improvement and Modernization Act (P.L.108-173).This 'insurance' costs Medicare enrollees' monthly premiums if they choose to have the plan.
  - Medigap-a private insurance that supplements the gaps that Parts A or B does not

cover. It is regulated by the Federal government.

- Also, in 1965 under Title XIX of the Social Security Act, Medicaid was established. This program was designed with an emphasis on dependent children and their mother, the disabled, and the elderly as an entitlement program. This program is funded by the federal and state governments. The following list tells of those who are eligible for this insurance as it pertains to children and their grandparents.
- Individuals who meet the requirement for Aid to Families with Dependent Children (AFDC).
- Recipients of adoption or foster care assistance under Title IV of the Social Security Act.
- All children born after September 30, 1983 who are under age 19, in families with incomes at or below the Federal Poverty Level (FPL).
- Children under 6 whose family is at or below 133% of the FPL
- "Optional targeted low-income children" (Longest, 2006) included within the State Children's Health Insurance Program (SCHIP) as established by the Balanced Budget Act of 1997 (P.L.105-33).
- Certain Medicare beneficiaries

- Social Security Income recipients.

Chart: Longest, Beaufort, 2008.

- The Older Americans Act of 1965 (P.L. 89-73) Congress enacted this bill to benefit the elderly to find community resources. An Administration on Aging was established and programs specifically targeted to the elderly were to be administered through state agencies.
- In 1974 The Child Abuse and Treatment Act (P.L.108-36) created the exclusive legislation dedicated to the precautionary analysis, recognition, and behavior towards child abuse.
- In 1975 The Social Services Block Grant (P.L. 97-35) or Title XX provides federal funds for states, and the states are given flexibility on how they are distributed and used by Social Services agencies. The funds are for low-income children, families, and adults for child care, child welfare and services to the elderly.
- In 1978 The Indian Child Welfare Act (P.L. 95-608) was legalized to recognize placing foster children with their own relatives.
- In 1980 The Adoption Assistance and Child Welfare Act (P.L. 96-272) created a "new Title IX-E Foster Care and Adoption assistance entitlement program" (CWLA, 2008). However, the wording was so ambiguous that states interpreted the law to mean that biological families were to be kept together –no matter what. This generated

problems within the adoption process. Other problems within the foster care system impeded the adoption of special needs children. This bill was allegedly to protect abused and neglected children and encouraged grandparents and relative care.

- In 1993 The Family Preservation and Support Services Program (P.L.103-66) was approved and amended Title V-B of the Social Security Act. This act gave states the auspices to create family focused programs for those children at risk, and families. It required states to plan more amenable outreach programs to support and preserve the family and protect the child. This bill broadened the definition of family to include people needing services regardless of family arrangements whether biological, adoptive or foster, extended or self-defined (U.S. Department of Health and Human Services, 2008). This act also encouraged states to improve interstate and intrastate cooperation to coordinate state service agencies and fund preventative services in the welfare system.
- In 1994 The Social Security Act (P.L. 103-432) or The Welfare Indicators Act set the federal government accountable for the degree at which families depend on welfare and its' programs. For the education and job skills of individuals (on welfare) are to become independent of the welfare system and strengthen families by insuring that children grow up in strong families.

- In 1996 The Personal Responsibility and Work Opportunity Act (P.L. 104-193) or the Welfare Reform Act was signed into law by President Clinton. This act replaced AFDC with Temporary Assistance for Needy Families (TANF) block grant. It ended welfare as an entitlement program and required recipients to get employment after two years of receiving benefits. After five years of benefits (one's lifetime limit) the federal government is finished funding the recipient. Finally, two parent families are encouraged and out of wedlock births are discouraged. Low-income children and their caregivers are not guaranteed income leaving the grandchild and grandparents in an awkward position. The grandparent is completely financially responsible for the upbringing of the grandchildren.

- In 1997 The Adoption and Safe Families Act (P.L. 105-89) was signed into law by President Clinton. This bill clarified the Adoption Assistance and Child Welfare Act of 1980. It created an agenda "...for moving children to permanency, provides adoption bonuses for states, and continues the child welfare waiver demonstrations. The law also renames The Family Preservation and Family Support programs to Promoting Safe and Stable Families, and expands the use of funds to two additional categories of service time-limited reunification services and adoption promotion as support services" (CWLA, 2008). Children's health and safety were the focus not the biological parents. Regardless of the parents level of abuse "…some families simply cannot and should not be kept together" (U.S. Department of Health and Human Services, 2008). This comment was made by Republican Senator John H. Chafee of Rhode Island. This bill changed the United States adoption and foster care system.

At that time First Lady of the United States Hillary Clinton exposed the orphaned issue since 1995, met with the Department of Health and Human Services to find out policy issues and make recommendations, and found a compromise between Republicans and Democrats in negotiations in Congress.

- The National Family Caregiver Support Act of 2000 "reconfirmed the Older Americans Act thus the NFCS which allows states to use up to 10% of their NFCS Program funds to asset older relative caregiver" (U.S. Department of Health and Human Services, 2008).
- On May 10, 2005 Senator Hillary Clinton introduced the Kinship Caregiver Support Act (S.985) to the Senate. This bill helps children being raised by grandparents to acquire the assistance they need and the grandparents receive assistance for the subsidized guardianship programs. Also, they can navigate a kinship navigator program to acquire their information to

meet the needs of the children or the grandparent.

This Kinship Navigator program will be administered by the Assistant Secretary for Children and Families within the Department of Health and Human Services and is required to consult periodically with the Assistant Secretary for Aging within the Department of Health and Human Services.

Unfortunately, the bill has not been approved by the Senate and is a dead bill. However, it was a precursor to other bills that were similar in content.

- In 2006 The Medicaid, Medicare, and SCHIP Indian Health Care Improvement Act provided for quality healthcare and outreach programs by creating an incentive for Indian healthcare providers to join the network. This bill also requires reporting data on Indians served the quality of healthcare, and how well health facilities are being upgraded.

- In 2006, The Improving Outcomes for Children Affected by Meth Act reauthorized and improved the Promoting Safe and Stable Families program (Senate opening statement, 2006) which links children with mentors in the community.

- Also in 2006 The Lifespan Respite Care Act (P.L. 109-442) was signed into law in December, 2006. This is a federal kinship navigator program and Congress is responsible for the funding.

- On February 16, 2007 Senator Hillary Clinton proposed The Kinship Caregiver Support Act (S. 661) in Congress. The bill has been introduced and read to the Senate and twice read to the Committee of Finance. Briefly, this bill establishes a Kinship Navigator program and creates guardianship assistance for children and those in foster care. Also, it ensures notice to grandparents and relatives when the children are entering foster care.

Both S.661/H.R.2188 were bipartisan legislation.

On May 7, 2007 Representative Danny K. Davies sponsored and introduced to the House, The Kinship Caregiver Support Act (H.R. 2188). This bill had two additional provisions over what S.661 had. Grandparents and other relatives raising children receive the help they need through the Promoting Safe and Stable Families Program. "Those children in foster care and families considering guardianship are made aware of the full range of permanency options and supports for children and guardians" (Children's Defense Fund, 2007).

10

Policy Analysis and Recommendations

"...changes in child welfare policies, family life and related social trends" (Smith, Beltran, Butts, & Kingson, 2000, p82) could be the reason why many grandchildren are living with their grandparents.

Good health and longevity allows grandparents to have a better quality of life than in prior years. A grandparents' grandchild being threatened whether emotionally, psychologically, or physically is intolerable.

Grandparents and relatives who care for children are not doing anything extraordinary. These mature adults are merely making up for a deficiency in the familial unit and going on with their lives while taking the grandchildren 'under their wing'. Grandparents and relatives have been raising their kin since time began, to provide a safe haven for their grandchildren or kin.

This societal shift of bringing both opposing generations together is an idea whose time has come.

Intergenerational communication and interaction between the generations never should have broken down. These artificial barriers have been created in society and it is time to tear those barriers down.

Policy is and will remain evolving so both opposing generations can share their resources intergenerationally.

The legislative shift in grandparent and grandchild care began in 1978 when The Indian Child Welfare Act approved of placements for relatives when placing foster children. In 1979 Miller vs. Yoakim took back the ability of the state to deny federal foster care payments under Title IV E of the Social Security Act. This established that grandparents and kin raising children cannot rely upon the state for qualifying for foster care rates. This left grandparents in financial need to raise their grandchildren.

The 1980 Adoption Assistance and Child Welfare Act encouraged grandparents and kin caring for their children that the child was supposed to be placed with the biological family.

The 1996 Personal Responsibility and Work Opportunity Act or the Welfare Reform Act cut off federal funding for grandparents and their grandchildren; it was no longer an entitlement program. An adopted child could only receive a grant through TANF (Temporary Assistance for Needy Families) if the grandparents had not received this grant in prior years. This brought the two opposing generations closer together because the grandparent and grandchildren needed to be living under one roof to survive. The time–limited benefits, and the demands to go back to work, causes a grandparent raising grandchildren to remain living together with their grandchildren.

The 1997 Adoption and Safe Families Act may further have encouraged grandparent and relative care by focusing on the child's welfare and not the biological parents. The child can be placed in a proper home (and the state receives a financial incentive for this adoption).

Now with the Kinship Caregiver Support Act of 2007, grandparents receive their help in caring for their grandchildren. As a result, the grandchild in return reaps the benefits of a fit and stable environment and home.

With all the technical information the professional gives, there is one very obvious and easily obtainable piece of information available to the grandparent. The grandparent is in a 'tailspin' and their life is turned around. The grandparent needs to gain control of the situation and the internet is the most immediate answer to empower the older surrogate parent. A good place to start would be at www.AARP.org. There is a wealth of information for the grandparent who finds they are going to have to deal with this type of situation. There are links to other websites around the country and outside of the country. There is a rationale there could be information available, another point of view. Information about this type of dilemma should not be limited to grandfamilies,

Children's networks have a vast quantity and quality of information such as, www.CWLA.org. There are legal websites, family websites, health websites and the list is endless. If a grandparent does not have a computer at home there are computers available in senior centers, libraries, some religious organizations, vocational services, law libraries, etc. The more information the grandparent obtains, the more empowered they become this leaves the grandparent in control and able to cope.

"Whatever the motive, the growing awareness of grandparents raising grandchildren seems to have emerged at the right time, providing an ideal issue for forging an intergenerational policy agenda and coalition" (Smith, Beltran, Butts, & Kingson, 2000, p 85). The intergenerational pairing seems to be beneficial politically, economically, societally, demographically, culturally, and ethnically. Intergenerational, Child Welfare, Medicare, Medicaid, SCHIP and Aging policies seem to be merging for the benefit of this special population. There is a definite evolving of policies. Everyday this unique population of opposite generations grows and merges, and their numbers cannot be ignored. The child in the genesis of their youth and the elder in the fall of their years, are setting a powerful statement to society. Maybe, there is something crucial these contrasting generations are trying to say.

Shouldn't we listen?

References

American Association of Retired Persons. (2007, October). *State fact sheets for grandparents and relatives raising children.* Retrieved January 21, 2008, from
http://www.grandfactsheets.org/state_fact_sheeta.cfm

American Association of Retired Persons.(2008) *Help for grandparents raising grandchildren.* Retrieved from, January 28, 2008, from
http://www.aarp.org/families/grandparents/raising_
grandchild/public_benefits_guide.html?print=yes

Barth, R.P.(2008). *Adoption.* In the encyclopedia of social work (Vol. 1,48-58). Washington, DC: Oxford University Press.

Brown-Standridge,M.D. (2000, April). *Healing bittersweet legacies: revisiting contextual family therapy for grandparents raising grandchildren in crisis.* Retrieved May 2, 2008, from
http://findarticles.com/articles/mi_qa_3658/is_2000
04/ai_n88821491.

Bryson, K. & Casper, L.M. (1999, May). *Co-resident Grandparents and grandchildren.* Retrieved on December 10, 2007, from
http://www.census.gov/pro/99pubs/p23-198.pdf.
U.S. Census Bureau, Washington, DC.

Caputo, R.K. (July, 2001).Grandparents and co-resident grandchildren in a youth cohort. *The Journal of Family Issues, 22(5) 541-556.*

Casper, L.M. & Bryson, K.R. (1998, March). *Co-resident grandparents and their grandchildren: grandparent maintained families.* Retrieved on December 10, 2007, from http://www.census.gov/population/www.document ation/twps0026/tw... U.S. Census Bureau: Washington,DC.

Child Welfare League of America.(2008).*Timeline of major child welfare legislation.* Retrieved on June 30, 2008, from http://www.cwla.org/advocacy/financing time-line.htm

Child Welfare League of America.(2008).*Summary of the kinship caregiver support act (s.985).* Retrieved June 30, 2008, from http://cwla.org/advocacy/summarykinshipact.htm

Child Welfare League of America.(2008).*National fact sheet for 2008.* Retrieved from http://www.cwla.org?advocacy/nationalfactsheet08 .htm

Child Welfare League of America.(2008).*Brief history of federal child welfare financing legislation.* Re-

trieved June 30, 2008, from
http:/www.cwla.org/advocacy/financinghistory.htm

Child Welfare League of America.(2008). *Summary of the Adoption and Safe families act of 1997.* Retrieved June 19, 2008, from
http:www.cwla.org/advocacy/asfapL105-89summary.htm

Dellman-Jenkins, M., Blankmeyer, M.. and Olesh, M. (2002). Adults in expanded grandparent roles: considerations for practice, policy, and research. *Educational Gerontology, 28, 219-235*

Edwards, O.W. (2003). Living with grandma: a grandfamily study. *School Psychology International, 204-217*

Fitzgerald, M. L. (2001). Grandparent's parents: intergenerational surrogate parenting.

Journal of Holistic Nursing, 19(3), 355-379
Force, L.T., Botsford, A Pisano, P.Λ., and Holbert, Λ. (2001). Grandparents raising grandchildren with and without a developmental disability: preliminary comparisons.

Journal of Gerontological Social Work, 33(4), 5-26.
Frank, J. (1999). *Elder Law in Maryland (2nd ed).* VA: Lexis Publishing.

Frolick, L. A. (1999). *Aging and the law: an interdisciplinary reader.* (Frolik, ed.). PA: Temple University Press.

Generations United. (2002) *Reaching across the ages: an active agenda to strengthening communities through intergenerational shared sites and resources.* Washington DC, Author, 1-30.

Goodman, C.C. (2007).Intergenerational triads on skipped generation grandfamilies. *The International Journal of Aging and Human Development, 65(3), 231-258.*

Goodman, C.C. (2007).Family dynamics in three generation grandfamilies. *Journal of Family Issues, 28(355),355-379*

Gov.Track.U.S. S.661-110th Congress. (2007).*Kinship caregiver support act.* Retrieved on April 28, 2008, from http://www.govtrack.us/congress/billtext.xpd?bills =siio-661

Grandfamilies. (2008). *Adoption.* Retrieved July 12, 2008, from http://www.grandfamilies.org/scripts/analysistab.cf m?topicID=13&printit=1

Grandfamilies. (2008). *Education:Narrative Analysis.* Retrieved July 12, 2008, from

http://www.grandfamilies.org/scripts/analysistab.cf
m?topicID=20&printit=J

Grandfamilies. (2008).*Financial Assistance.* Retrieved
July 12, 2008, from
http://www.grandfamilies.org/scriptsanalysistab.cf
m?topicID=74&printit=1

Grandfamilies. (2008). *Relative foster care.* Retrieved
on July 12, 2008, from
http://www.grandfamilies.org/scripts/analysistab.cf
m?topicID=42&printit=1

Grandfamilies. (2008). *About Granfamilies.* Retrieved
on July 12, 2008, from
http://www.grandfamilies.org/scripts/analysistab.cf
m?topicID=26&printit=1

Grandfamilies. (2008). *Subsidized guardianship.* Retrieved July 12, 2008, from
http://www.grandfamilies.org/scripts/analysistab.cf
m?topicID=42&printit=1

H.R.2188. (2007,September). *Kinship caregiver support act.* Retrieved April 30, 2008, from
http://Thomas.loc.gov/cgi-
bin/bdquery/z?d110:HR02188:@@@D&summ2=
m&

Kausler, D.H. & Kausler, B.(1996).*The Graying of America*. Chicago: University of Illinois, pp.147-148.

Kelch-Oliver, K. (2008). African American grandparent caregivers: stresses and implications for counselors. *The Family Journal,16(43), 43-50.*

Kivnick, H. & Sinclair, H.M. (1996).Grandparenthood. In *The encyclopedia of gerontology.* (Vol.1, pp.611-624).New York: Acedemic Press.

Kluger, M.P. & Aprea, D.M.(1999). Grandparents raising grandchildren: a description of the families and a special pilot program. *Journal of Gerontological Social Work, 32(!),5-17.*

Lugaila, T. & Overturf, J. (2004, March).*Children and the households they live in:*
   2000. Retrieved December 10, 2007, from http://www.census.gov/prod/2004pub/censr-14.pdf U.S. Census Bureau, Washington,DC

Mills, T.L., Gomez-Smith, Z. & DeLeon, J.M. (2005). Skipped generation families: sources of psychological distress among grandmothers of grandchildren who live in homes where neither parent is present. *The Marriage and Family Review, 37:1/2,191-212*

Minkler, M. & Fuller-Thomson, E.(2005). African-American grandparents raising grandchildren: a national study using the census 2000 American Community Survey. *The Journal of Gerontology,60B:2, s82-s92.*

National Association of Area Agencies on Aging.(2002). *Promising Practices in Encouraging and supporting grandparents and relatives raising children.* Washinton DC.

National Human Services Assembly.(2007). *Strenghening grandfamilies through respite care: policy brief # 20.* Washington, DC.

Opening statement on Medicare, Medicaid, & SCHIP and the Indian Health Care Improvement Act of 2006. (2006,June 8). Retrived June 4, 2008,from http://64.233.169.104/search?Q=cache: fQsQYgFlazgJ:www.senate.gov/=finance/hearings/ statements106080...

Olsen, S. (2008). *The reality of kinship care of relative children.* Retrieved July 14, 2008, from http://www.solutionsforchildrenandcaregivers.com/ 573.html

Pearson, J.L.,Hunter,A.G., Cook, J.M., Ialongo, N.S. & Kellam, S.G. (1997). Grandmother involvement in child caregiving in an urban community. *The Gerontologist, 37(5), 650-657.*

Sands, R.G. & Goldberg-Glen, R.S.(2000). *Factors associated with stress among grandparents raising their grandchildren.* The National Council on Family Relations. 49:1, 97-105.

Scarcella, C.A., Macomber, J.E. & Geen, R. (2003). *Identifying and addressing the needs of children in grandparents care.*The Urban Institute. B-55, 1-10.

Simmons, T. & Dye, J. 1.(2003). *Grandparents living with the children: 2000.* Retrieved on December 10, 2007, from http://www.census.gov?prod?2003pubs/c2kbr-31.pdf. U.S. Census Bureau, Washington,DC.

Smith, C.J. Beltran, A., Butts, D. & Kingson, E.R. (2000). Granparents raising grandchildren: emerging program and policy issues for the 21st century. *Journal of Gerontological Social Work ,34:1, 81-94.*

The Social Security Administration.(2008).*The Social Security Act of 1935.* Retrieved on July 14, 2008, from http://www.ssa.gov/history/35acti.html

Somary, K. & Stricker, G.(1998). Becoming a grandparent : a longitudinal study of expectations and early experiences as a function of sex and lineage. *The Gerontologist, 38:1, 81-94.*

References

Szinovacz, M. E. (1998). Grandparents Today: a demographic profile. *The Gerontologist, 38:1, 37-52.*

U.S. Census Bureau.(2003). *Grandparents: American Community Survey..* Retrieved June 2, 2008, from http://factfinder.census.gov/servelet/STTable?_bm =y&-geo_id=0100...

U.S. Census Bureau.(2004). *Grandparents: American community survey.* Retrived on June 2, 2008, from http://factfinder.census.gov/servlet/STTable?_bm= y&-geo_id=0100

U.S.Census Bureau. (2005). *Grandparents: 2005 American community survey.* Retrived on June 2, 2008, From http://factfinder.census.gov/servelet/STTable?_bm =y&-geo_id==0100

U.S. Census Burcau. (2006). *Grandparents: American community survey.* Retrieved on June 2, 2008, from http://factfinder.census.gov/servelet/STTable?_bm =y&-geo_id=0100

U.S. Census Bureau. (2006). *American community sur-vey percentage of grandparents responsible for their grandchildren .* Retrieved on December 10, 2007, from http://factfinder.census.gov/servelet/ThematicMap Frameset.Servelet?...

U.S.Census Bureau. (2006). *Percent of grandparents responsible for their grandchildren: 2006.* Retrieved on October18, 2007, from http://factfindercensus. gov/servelet/GRTTable?bm=y&-geo_id=010

The Welfare Indicators Act of 1994. (1997). *The welfare indicators act of 1994.*Retrieved on June 19, 2008, from http://aspe.os.dhas.gov/hsp/indicators 97/chap 4.htm

Woodworth,R.S., Debelko,H. &Hollidge,M. (1998). *Respite services to support grandparents raising grandchildren.* Retrived July 14, 2008,from http://www.archrespite.org